THE MIND A.

What do I say about the mind apart from; it is confusing, complex, elusive, cannot be controlled, extremely powerful, negative, sensual, sexual, a dictator, controlling, different from the body, and spirit.

The mind is a powerful tool that have access to all, yet; very little is known about the mind apart from what is written in textbooks.

Listen, I am not one to research what others say and tell. My knowledge base is truly different yet, at times I feel trapped in a body that I truly do not want to be in due to limitations; barriers set up by my mind; me. Therefore, for me, and to me, the mind is an independent source of energy that do block you from attaining your full spiritual sense; potential here on Earth. People talk about Universal Energy – the Universe but, do they truly know the Universe, and the true power that is out there?

Before I fully get into this book, I need you to do something for me.

I need you to go to YouTube and pull up; *ONE DROP by Robert Nesta Marley aka, Bob Marley.*

Listen to what he said in the beginning of the song when he said; *"THEY MAKE THEIR WORLD SO HARD, EVERY DAY WE GOT TO KEEP ON FIGHTING. THEY MADE THEIR WORLD SO HARD EVERY DAY THE PEOPLE ARE DYING."*

Now, with this Pandemic:

"WHO ARE THE ONES DYING?"
"WHO ARE THE ONES STARVING?"

"WHO ARE THE ONES THAT CANNOT PAY THEIR BILLS?"

"WHO ARE THE ONES WHO ARE HOMELESS?"

"WHO ARE THE ONES THAT ARE JOBLESS?"

"HOW MANY OF YOU HAVE TO CLOSE DOWN YOUR BUSINESS DUE TO "POLITICAL LIES, CORPORATE LIES AND GREED," PHARMACEUTICAL GREED, POLITICAL; GOVERNMENTAL GENOCIDE; THE VIRUSES DEVELOPED AND MANUFACTURED IN LABORATORIES THAT KILL YOU THE CITIZENS OF THE LAND THUS, ENDANGERING YOUR LIFE, AND YES, KILLING YOU?"

"HOW MANY OF YOU HAVE AND HAS LOST YOUR CHILDREN, MOTHER, FATHER, BROTHER, GRANDPARENTS, FRIENDS, AND FOES TO COVID-19?"

"HOW MANY OF YOU ARE BLAMING THE CHINESE YET, CANNOT SEE THE ENTIRE/WHOLE VACCINE SCAM?"

"IS THIS NOT THE SAME THING THEY (AMERICA – WHITE PEOPLE) DID TO AFRICANS WHEN IT CAME TO AIDS AND EBOLA?"

"IS THIS NOT THE SAME AS THEIR TUSKEGEE EXPERIMENT ON BLACK AMERICANS AND SYPHILIS – THE DISEASE THE UNITED STATES GOVERNMENT DESIGNED AND MANUFACTURED IN LABS, AND DID INFECT MANY IN THE BLACK COMMUNITY WITH?"

Let me not talk about the "different pharmaceuticals that screw up your internal organs," cocaine, crack cocaine, alcohol, the different arms, psychological brainwashing, and more.

Now. Look at the Global Marketplace.

Who is being shut down yet, the government officials, corporate greed – corporate owners, Pharmaceutical Greed – Demons, and their employees are still working, travelling, eating well, collecting their hefty salaries; paycheques, and more?

Now. Look at the Pharmaceutical Giants; Demons, and so-called 1% yes, _the SOULLESS._

Now are they hurting financially?

Now tell me, are they taking their own drugs meant for you?

Now tell me. _"ARE HUMANS NOT THE SACRIFICE FOR WHO CONTROL THEM; YOU?"_

Therefore, Black People, wake up, and grow up. Stop letting the GUILTY CONTROL AND KILL YOU. Listen, the Death of DMX should serve, and be a warning unto many of you but, like ignorant fools you've all going to ignore what is happening – really happening to the Black Race Mentally, Physically, Financially, Health Wise, Spiritually, Environmentally, God Wise, and More. Look deeper because, many know the truth of the Music and or Entertainment Industry thus, MANY BLACKS ARE SACRIFICED – HAVE TO DIE. Many have not their own life. All *that is given is taken away via drugs, unhealthy lifestyle, and more. Abrahamic Law of Human and Animal Sacrifice.*

And I am not going to say anymore because; "*Blacks are going to feel it wicked and rude if you don't wake up and start doing for self.*"

Stop depending on the White Race for Financial Stability, your health woes, a home, your day to day living, a god, and more. Contrary to your beliefs, many if not all of humanities health woes has and have to do with White People and the germs – viruses, and diseases they design and manufacture in labs.

Listen. *THE WHITE RACE IS THE GUILTY RACE.* This Bob Marley told you in his song *GUILTINESS.* Therefore, beware of wolves; the White Race that come in Sheep Clothing.

As Bob said; "*THE BREAD THEY EAT IS SORROW,*" and he's infinitely correct. Therefore, *GUARD YOUR LIFE HERE ON EARTH AND IN THE SPIRITUAL REALM.*

Tell me now. "*ARE YOU NOT THE PROFIT AND PROPHETS OF THOSE WHO WANT TO ANNIHILATE YOU?*"

Now let me ask you this.

All the ills happening here on Earth:

"WAS THIS APART OF GOD'S PLAN?"

OR

"WAS IT NOT THE PLAN OF MAN?"

Those who *"KILL AT WILL,"* and get away with it daily because humans; us as humans, *let our enemies get away with "MURDER."*

Thus, I refuse what they want me to be.

BABYLON SYSTEM by Robert Nesta Marley aka, Bob Marley.

I refuse to die along side the White Race of Demons that live to kill and do kill daily, and you the *FOOLS OF THE WORLD* cannot see that this "FALLEN RACE" has and have not only deceived the lots of you, but; *has, and have locked billions of you in hell.*

Thus, Bob Marley told you, and Peter Tosh told you in his song VAMPIRE.

It's time now for every nation – you the citizens to rebel and take back control of your life if you want to live – escape hell.

Listen, the White Race truly do not know the Hell that awaits them Spiritually, and universally. Allelujah

I know therefore, I see; can tell you of what I see.

Onwards I go with this book.

But, do they; these people truly know how to attain peace – true peace?

Do they know how to attain the power of the Universe?

Do they truly know how to surround self with peace – true peace?

Do they know how, and truly know how to wrap that peace – true peace; Energy Source around them so that they are in a different world void of the ills that surround them, and face them here on Earth?

Do you as an individual even know these things?
Do you have true peace in your life?

Can you attain that true peace you need in your life?

Do you even think of the mind, and how the mind control your thoughts, sleep, the things you do, the shaping and manipulation of your life, and more?

Can you even shut your mind down so that the mind do not think for you, and you do the thinking for yourself?

Many questions yes, yet; the answers are few because; the mind is that elusive and complex in many ways. Therefore, we truly do not know how the mind work when it comes to the Physical, and Spiritual.

Yes, for some this is simple, but what I am talking about is truly not simple but complex because; *absolutely no one can shut the mind off just like that.* The mind chatters, *and the mind is a master of deception.* Thus, Negative and Positive Energy comes from the mind; flow through the human body, encompass Earth, and more.

Therefore, our spirit is caged in the confines of the body – our flesh for a time.

Through The Roots feat. Lutan Fyah – AT PEACE

Right now, I truly do not want or need to be anyone in the White Race because; *the darkness above them, and around them wow.*

I know for a fact without doubt that this race – *THE WHITE RACE CANNOT BE SAVED.* Hell, and the Universe awaits them patiently. The lies they've told on the Universe, Outer Space, God – the True God of Life, Genetics, Earth, the Different Races; Nations, and more has and have locked them out of

Life – All Life except for Hell. There are no ands, ifs, or buts about this. *see MINI BOOK*

It's March 25, 2021 and I started this book over a weak ago but, did not get far because I needed to complete my book, *I NEED ANSWERS GOD* for which is complete now. I just have to upload it – this book on Lulu.com.

Further, I was not, and I am still not sure if I want or need to include dreams in this book, but what would this book be without dreams – that which I see via my dream world literally.

Thus, *the darkness I dreamt in the sky when it comes to White People, and their lies about other planets.* Yes, total darkness; then dots of light, but not light. In the darkness there were white dots. Yes, like the dot of a period.

I will not analyze this dream because I truly do not think this race can come out of their darkness due to ancestral lies, murder, rape, theft, genocide, just all out demonic and evil way of doing things. Plus, the lies they tell on God whether subliminally and or, through the way they write. You cannot tell people God say one thing then go back on his word and say another thing. This is truly not fair or just to God. Nor is this fair and just to humans. Therefore, as humans; we should know that it is in fact *"demons"* *– the Children and People of Demons – Satan that wrote the bible to get you confused as well as, get you* *to sin so you – your spirit can go to hell to die a brutal death.*

Listen, the more we as humans Sin here on Earth, is the longer your spirit stay burning in the confines of your hell in Hell.

Plus, the more you Sin here on Earth, is the longer Death and the Demons of Hell stay alive in Hell.

So

<u>SINS IS TIME – MORE TIME ADDED UNTO THE LIFE OF DEATH IN THE REALM OF DEATH – HELL.</u>

So yes, it's humans that give Life and Rise to Death Physically, and Spiritually. No, not Universally because, the Universe cannot die.

Thus, in his song *"ONE LOVE"* Bob Marley asked; *"is there a place for the hopeless sinner who has hurt all mankind just to save his own?"* And the answer to his question is <u>*yes.*</u> That place is <u>*Hell.*</u>

So, as the White Race has and have sinned, they truly do not know what awaits them, but I do. Thus, there are <u>*NO DO OVERS IN LIFE OR DEATH.*</u>

Therefore, *'THE LIFE YOU LIVE HERE ON EARTH DETERMINES WHERE YOU GO ONCE THE SPIRIT SHED THE FLESH.'*

As humans we truly do not think of our Spiritual Self.

Did I dream about Ika and Demitri the YouTube Vlogger?

Yes.

Demitri went back to Greece by himself in the dream, and I found their home and chastised Ika for allowing Demitri to go back to Greece by himself. You know what, let me leave this dream alone because when I went into the home, I saw this young child – female with get black shoulder length hair that was curled. I thought wow, when did they have a child but, *the little girl was not real.* I say not real because, I do not know how to explain it. The young girl ended up being Ika's son. The little one not her eldest child and or, son. In the dream, I called him Joshua and or, Joseph but the name began with a J. I can't remember if it was Joshua or Joseph I called him, and he answered and said yes.

Further, in the dream, Demitri was a good father and I told Ika this. In the dream Demitri bonded nicely to her last child – son and you saw this in the dream.

What got to me in the dream was the floor of their Condo how it was unkept as well as, this old cream phone receiver that was on the floor lying/laying up.

Wow, I told you the entire dream. So, something is truly not right with these two because their world is a façade it seems, and the problem in the dream was not Demitri but Ika. She needs to clean herself, and her home up period. Ole people sey, ole fiya stick easily lit. So Ika, whatever you are doing, it is being seen. So, clean yourself up. Your home is too damned dirty.

So, with that said, I truly do not know what to write now because the Spiritual Realm is different. There are so many people out there claiming the Universe, and I don't even know if claiming the Universe is the correct wording.

Many people do look to the Universe for Power, Spiritual Healing, Spiritual Help, Spiritual Wealth, A Mate, and more. I know the unlimited power that is out there that can be had but, attaining this power at times, I truly do not want or need. Yes, I would use this for the better good, but without Truth, *the Truth of God in the Midst holding my hand to create and do good, what is the point?*

So, know. There is unlimited power out there to be had. This power is what Evil seek; need.

If Evil get this power; then, nothing could or would stop Evil from creating and destroying at will; then creating again and destroying at will again.

Evil would not, and cannot die if Evil had this unlimited Power.

Listen, when it comes to certain things with God, I am a hopeless romantic. Hey, I truly like to hold hands and God is no exception to my holding hands with. And no, I truly do not want or need to hold the hands of everyone. I am truly selective and picky with who I hold hands with. If I truly don't like you, or like you, I will not hold hands with you and even if I like you, or truly like you, I truly will not hold hands with you. You have to be truly special in my world and book for me to hold hands with you.

Yes, picky and funny me. But this is me. I am me, and you are you.

As humans, we know a lot more about the Physical than we do about the Spiritual. For some, the Spiritual is complex, but the Spiritual is truly not complex. It is because we do not know the Spiritual that we think the Spiritual is complex. There's a lot that I truly do not know about the Spiritual hence God to me limits me.

We know about God and the Physical and I did touch base on this in one of my very, very earlier books. But, _did you know that there is a REALM BEYOND GOD?_

Yes, this Realm is dangerous thus, not many people know about this realm, and other realms where God truly do not exist. No, don't let your mouth drop open and say, "I am a psychopath that do not know anything." *I am telling you there are different realms out there.* The Realm Beyond God, and the REALM WHERE GOD TRULY DO NOT EXIST.

Listen, the Physical and Spiritual Realm are baby steps towards finding and knowing the truth. If God did not want me to know about the different realms out there, God would not have opened my eyes to the truth, nor would God show me and or, tell me of these realms, and the danger of the REALM BEYOND GOD.

The Spiritual Realm is extremely powerful therefore, you have to know how to walk spiritually.

There is a PHYSICAL LIFE AND DEATH, AND A SPIRITUAL LIFE AND DEATH. This Spiritual Life and Death, and Physical Life and Death is determined by you the individual. Thus, "*THE LIFE YOU LIVE HERE ON EARTH DETERMINES WHERE YOU GO ONCE YOUR SPIRIT SHED THE FLESH,*" and I've told you this in numerous books.

I don't know if I should say this. And truly forgive me Mother Earth but, the Flesh is a prison for the Spirit in my view.

Meditation
Transcendental Meditation
Thought Transference

Unlimited Power
Hearing the thoughts and conversation of others
Every aspect of Meditation
Mind Control

Wow.

To me and for me, <u>*MEDITATION TRULY DO NOT*</u> <u>*WORK.*</u>

<u>*ABSOLUTELY NO ONE CAN CONTROL THE*</u> <u>*MIND.*</u> The mind will forever control you because, <u>*within the human body there are different spirits.*</u>

And I am going to leave you to think.

Michelle

KEEP THINKING

YES, KEEP THINKING

Yes, I am travelling. Well, my mind is travelling to Nevis and St. Kitts.

Told Lovey I am leaving him for Nevis and St. Kitts. Saw the perfect place in Nevis where I want to live. The greenery awed me so much that I left Lovey for real. Well for the moment.

Trust me, if I could move to Nevis with that type of greenery – beauty, I would be in paradise; my paradise with God. I would have no need to bug Lovey for a home, and a beautiful place to stay; live.

Michelle

YES, KEEP THINKING

Okay, why did I do that?

To show you that absolutely no one can control their mind. The mind will not allow you to fully and totally control it. Thus, _the mind is truly powerful._

Now, how many of you were travelling to Nevis and St. Kitts with me?

How many of you thought of me and my journey?

Be truthful now.

Thus, my True Loved Ones. True and good blessings bestowed upon you all the time continually without end in goodness and in truth.

Well, people say meditation helps to control the mind. And I am telling you no one can control their mind in that way.

Well, meditation helps to calm the brain; mind.

Yes, but does meditation control the mind.

I have a high tolerance for pain.

That's good, but is that controlling your mind?

Listen, and listen to me carefully.

IF YOU CAN CONTROL YOUR MIND, YOU WOULD HAVE UNLIMITED POWER AND ALL ACCESS TO THE UNIVERSE, AND BEYOND.

YOU COULD CREATE PLANETS IF YOU CAN AND COULD CONTROL YOUR MIND.

IF YOU COULD CONTROL YOUR MIND, YOU WOULD NOT BE HERE ON PLANET EARTH. YOU WOULD BE SOMEPLACE ELSE.

IF YOU COULD CONTROL YOUR MIND, YOU WOULD KNOW HOW THE UNIVERSE WORK.

IF YOU COULD CONTROL YOUR MIND, THE KNOWLEDGE YOU WOULD HAVE WOW.

IF YOU COULD CONTROL YOUR MIND, YOU WOULD HAVE NO USE FOR THE FLESH.

IF YOU COULD CONTROL YOUR MIND, YOU WOULD HAVE NO USE FOR GOD.

Therefore, know the mind because; the mind houses different spirits, and the mind is that powerful.

The mind has and have its own chatter. Chatter that is truly not easily turned off. The mind also have/has its own *language.*

Therefore, *IF YOU COULD CONTROL YOUR MIND, YOU WOULD CONTROL EARTH, AND CHANGE THE ENVIRONMENT OF EARTH WITHOUT THE AIDE OF GOD, AND OTHER SPIRITUAL BEINGS THAT IS/ARE OUT THERE.*

IF YOU COULD CONTROL YOUR MIND, YOU WOULD CONTROL EVIL. MEANING, YOU WOULD BE ABLE TO STOP ALL FACETS OF EVIL HERE ON EARTH BECAUSE; YOU WOULD HAVE FULL CONTROL OF DEATH INCLUDING, FULL CONTROL OF FEMALE BLACK DEATH.

Now you have right and true knowledge. Yes, I am done, but; unfortunately, I cannot upload 8 pages at the time of writing this book on Lulu.com. I have to have more pages therefore I have to add fillers to this book.

Well, what about Spiritual Baths?

Does Spiritual Baths not cleanse you spiritually?

Spiritual Baths are good, and some baths make you feel lighter; your body feel lighter because; *the SPIRIT CAN GET TRULY HEAVY.*

When there is too much dead people around you, it does take a toll on your body therefore, your spirit let you know. The Spirit will make you feel that dead weight of self.

And yes, *DEAD WEIGHT* is a known fact for some in the Black Community if you know the dead in that way.

It's like some people who are carrying the Casket of the Dead. That dead person in the casket can let those people feel their weight.

Some, if the person is not being buried in the right spot – the spot they told you to bury them in before they died. Upon taking their body to its final resting place and or, place of internment, the spirit and or, the person in the casket will give you hell; a warm time when taking them to their final resting place and or, internment.

Well, when you die, the spirit leaves the flesh behind.

No, not fully.

Yes, the Spirit shed the Flesh but upon internment that spirit must find their body and or, source. And yes, I know I've just confused the heck out of you.

Know:
Your Spiritual Self is a reflection of your Physical Self, and your Physical Self is a reflection of your Spiritual Self here on Earth. But, this changes in time.

I am confusing you because it's hard for me to explain. So, let's leave it.

Just know. *If you are of Life, and you have more Good than Sin, when the time is right your Spirit have to; must change from its Physical Hue.* You know what, it's better if I told you face to face because writing what I need to say is hard.

So, if you see me, you can ask me all the questions you need answers for when it comes to the spirit. And yes, I hope I will be able to give you all the correct answers you need. And please, truly do not ask me to talk to your dead friend, dead family member, dead child or whatever. I do not speak to the dead in that way. Nor do I want to speak to the dead in that way. Too scary for me.

I truly love life and, I truly do not like to see lifeless bodies.

Now back to Spiritual Baths.

Having a Spiritual Bath truly do not cleanse your actual spirit. I truly do not know if I can draw on this analogy. And Lovey, forgive me if I am wrong.

Saying a Spiritual Bath fully cleanse your spirit is like saying all your sins are forgiven once you are baptized.

BAPTISM DO NOT CLEANSE YOU OF YOUR SINS. YOUR SINS ARE STILL ON YOUR SIN

RECORD AS UNFORGIVEN IF THE PERSON YOU'VE WRONGED; ERRED HAVE NOT FORGIVEN YOU. SO, TO SAY; "ALL YOUR SINS ARE WASHED AWAY – CLEANSED ONCE YOU ARE BAPTISED IS A LIE." You are lying on yourself and on God.

I've told you in other books. "GOD CANNOT FORGIVE YOU OF SINS YOU'VE DONE UNTO MATTHEW, HENRY, MR. SMITHE, MR. SMITH OR WHOMEVER. THE PERSON YOU WRONGED MUST FORGIVE YOU IN ORDER FOR THAT SIN TO BE TAKEN OFF YOUR SIN RECORD."

IF GOD FORGIVE YOU OF SINS DONE UNTO ANYONE THEN GOD WOULD BE OVERSTEPPING HIS OR HER BOUNDARIES. THUS, SINNING, AND TAKING AWAY THE RIGHT OF THE PERSON YOU ERRED AND OR, WRONGED.

I'VE TOLD YOU. "GOD CAN ONLY FORGIVE SINS DONE UNTO GOD."

So, Sister Pat, all the news carrying you do to Pastor against Sister Charmaine, you are held accountable for that. What Sister Charmaine do and does in her personal life is Sister Charmaine's business. Her sex life with her husband do not concern you because it's her that is married to him. Sister Charmaine did not marry you, her, and him. Sister Charmaine married him. So, however she throws it down on her husband is her and his way of her pleasing him; each other.

So yes, if Sister Charmaine cuss you out reckless and rude, and call you all the nasty names in the book then yes, she has a right to do so. You have no business in her Marital Life Sexually come on now.

The time you are there carrying news you would fix up your own home because; your home is as filthy and dirty as you. Allelujah

Wow, now I am off topic.

When it comes to the mind. Your gateway has and have moved. We do not secure our Gateway to Life, nor did we secure our gateway – Pathway to Life. *Soft Spot*

As we grow, we do not think of our Spiritual Well Being. All we think about is our Physical Well Being.

We do not think of what we consume – put in our body, food wise, thought wise, water wise, sexually, Sin Wise, and more.

All these things. The food we eat, sins we do; commit here on Earth, the water we drink, our thoughts, sex we have do affect our Spiritual Self. So, the more negative things we put in our body to harm the flesh,

<u>*the shorter our lifespan is here on Earth*</u> thus, the Spirit shedding the flesh.

Michelle

March 26, 2021 Dreams

Oh man I do not know what's going to happen to the Global Economy Job Wise when it comes to White People.

It's bad enough that we have this Pandemic where many businesses have and has gone under.

Many have and has lost their job – source of income.

Many ills is happening in certain family.

Many are discovering they have a home and family, but with all of this, I cannot worry.

This morning, *I dreamt White People and jobs.* Yesterday, I did dream about White People and Jobs, and today I am dreaming about them; White People and Jobs again. So, economically, I truly do not know about White Companies surviving on a whole globally.

Like I said, *darkness is around and or, in the sky when it comes to White People* thus, many truly do not have a home – place with God literally and truly. The damage has and have been done therefore, *God has and have locked them – the White Race out of the Realm and Kingdom of Life.* You cannot give the People of the Globe Death and expect them to live. *Absolutely no one can or will live.* They will die and this is what's happening here on Earth. Many live for

Death therefore, Death is given, and lives are taken Physically, and Spiritually.

So twice this morning I dreamt about Jobs when it came to the White Race. One particular dream had to do with me.

I was employed by this company – White Owned company. I did my job and did not socialize too much with anyone. This one White Manager; Female that was about 270 to 300 pounds and say, 5' 11" tall was the boss. She transferred this White Female to British Colombia I believe but one of the Provinces anyway. I believe the Female Boss had long brown hair and was wearing a red sweater. She didn't like sending her employee – Female Employee to British Colombia and or, another Province. I don't know if the girl she sent was her friend, but she did not have a family so relocating her was not an issue however, she did not like sending her to another Province. You could tell she had cried prior. Thus, you could see the nose naught on her red sweater. Going into her office she cried further and called the female employee that she had to relocate into her office.

I thought she was going to relocate me as well because, she came back out of her office a short time later and said, *"as for you, you are fired."* She began to explain to me that this White Employee – guy did not like me because I was not sociable. I told her; *"I did not come to work to be sociable, I came to work to work."*

Apparently, I was doing my job too well and he did not like that. I showed him up. She – the White Female Boss began to tell me about *my hair.* They did not like the way I had my hair and I told her, *"I am not going to change my hair to suit anyone, nor am I going to change myself for anyone."* This one Black Lady was there, and I asked her what was wrong with my hair. But as usual, Blacks in certain places do not stick up for their own. The money suit them fine therefore, *they go with the flow of WHITE SOCIETY AND WHAT WHITE PEOPLE TELL THEM IS THE NORM AND OR, STANDARD.*

Thus, I should not expect any better by House and Field Niggers that are bought and sold. Have to do the bidding of Massa because they have no balls or backbone. Thus, many have and has sold their soul for the dollar bill.

Further, many truly do not know that all the Children of God are Young Black Females with Kinky and or, Nappy, Happy as Pappy Hair with the exception of 1 bi-racial child. This is how I saw it, and this is how I am relating it back to you.

So, I truly do not know what is going on in the work force globally, but it's time Black People take a stand and stop changing them to *BECOME DEAD – WHITE. I refuse to change me or my kinky hair to please WHITE PEOPLE BECAUSE THEIR*

STANDARD OF BEAUTY IS TRULY NOT BEAUTY.

I REFUSE TO BE LIKE ANYONE WHITE OR BE WHITE. I AM OF LIFE AND I HAVE TO REPRESENT LIFE AND CONTINUE TO BE OF LIFE. THOSE IDIOTIC BLACK FOOLS THAT SEEK ACCEPTANCE FROM WHITES CAN DO AS THEY PLEASE, BUT I REFUSE TO. I AM NOT MENTALLY SICK, NOR DO I HATE MY BLACK SKIN, BLACK HAIR, BLACK GOD, BLACK LIFE, AND MORE. I HAVE TO RESPECT ME, MY BLACK GOD, MY BLACK CULTURE, MY BLACK HERITAGE, AND MORE.

F THOSE IN THE WHITE RACE THAT HATE ME AND MY COLOUR. YOUR JEALOUSY IS YOURS BECAUSE GOD PREFERRED US; THE BLACK RACE OVER YOU JUST TO BE A BIT RACIST.

I AM OF GOD. THEREFORE, I AM BLESSED AND HIGHLY FAVOURED. WHAT CAN YOU SAY?

DO NOT TELL ME WHAT LIFE IS BECAUSE NONE IN THE WHITE RACE KNOW WHAT LIFE TRULY IS.

NONE IN THE WHITE RACE KNOW WHO GOD TRULY IS. SO, TRULY DON'T WHEN IT COMES TO ME AND MY BLACKNESS BECAUSE; I WILL SCHOOL YOU, AND PUT YOU IN YOUR PLACE.

WHEN I CHANGE ME TO BE WHITE, I AM TELLING MY BLACK GOD – LIFE THAT I DO NOT RESPECT HIM OR HER.

WHEN I CHANGE ME TO BE WHITE, I AM TELLING MY BLACK GOD – LIFE THAT DEATH MEANS MORE TO ME THAN HIM AND OR, HER.

WHEN I CHANGE ME TO BE WHITE, I AM TELLING MY BLACK GOD – LIFE THAT I GIVE UP MY LIFE TO BECOME DEATH BECAUSE HE; MY BLACK GOD IS WORTHLESS – HATH NO VALUE TO ME ANYMORE. And truly do not go there with but above you gave up God for Nevis and St. Kitts due to beauty; greenery. The area that you would like to live in. So yes, something is truly not right when it comes to White Supervisors wanting Blacks to change them to look like them.

Absolutely no one should have to change them self to look like what their boss want or, need them to be. *As Blacks, we cannot live our life for the White Race. We have to live our life for self, and the goodness of self.*

We are not White. WE ARE BLACK. We have to live the Black Way and do all that is right for us; you as a person. Your hair and skin colour should not come down to what your boss say it is or should be.

No job should base your credentials on looks, hair texture, colour, colour of skin, colour of eyes, your sexuality, and more. Transgender It Things excluded. God is not abominable. Therefore, it is truly wise not to be around Abominations of Life. Therefore, *it is strictly forbidden for MEN TO WEAR WOMEN'S CLOTHING, AND VICE VERSA.*

So yes, you can say, as the Earth is different; diverse, so too is the Spiritual Realm.

Therefore, it's time *WHITES STOP IMPOSING THEIR NASTINESS AND NASTY WAYS ON BLACK PEOPLE.*

It's time for Blacks to wake up and see their own doom – demise because like I've told you in some of my other books:

"HELL IS FULL OF BLACK PEOPLE AND RECRUITING MORE."

The White Way of Life is truly not the Black Way of Life, and it's time we as

Black People realize this, and stop being fooled by people who truly do not like us.

People that their main goal is to see that Blacks Fail in Life and never Achieve God – their Black God ever again.

Listen, Lovey is my keep therefore, despite me saying I give up Lovey for Nevis and St. Kitts, I can't give up my truth come on now. Lovey is tied, glued to me and there are no ands, ifs, or buts about this. My relationship with Lovey is just that mine. Lovey know(s) me period. Therefore, we are more than solid and truthful in every way.

My other dream involved this Babylonian Indian and or, Hindu. No, I dreamt my brothers. I was at church it seems, and they came to get my key along with my brother's son. Mind you, I did not give it to them. They left, and I went after them to give them the key.

Then, I dreamt the Babylonian Indian and or, Hindu Male. He came to get me. He needed my help. Apparently, his spider got stuck in a Spider Web. So, going on the Veranda I saw the Spider and 2 Black Cats in the Spider Web. You could see the eyes of the Black Cats. The cats did not move and neither did the Spider.

Now, the Spider did not look like a spider. Think Sperm. The Spider looked like a Sperm to me. I believe I helped him to let the Spider lose but the

Spider did not fall on the ground. He said it was still asleep. Plus, he told me he wanted to change is clothing into a suit to be like other people. I know what this dream means.

The way the Black Cats were situated on the Spider Web is, the cats were hanging down from the top in the middle of the web, and the spider was below the cats as if coming up towards them.

Therefore, someone is my family is in great danger and I know who. He is a child that truly do not listen. Plus, more people are going to die in India – Asian Lands. *The suit that he was going to put on – wear.*

I will not worry about these dreams because evil will always be evil. And yes, Death will always show me Death because, *I am in the valley of Death – Earth.*

So yes, I am going to have to call my nephew and caution him.

I so do not know why the men in my family – my mother's grandchildren and great grandchildren have to be so dyam gullible. They don't take good and sound advice from the elders that are guiding them in the right direction.

I've been through hell and back. I know. But, you would figure the younger generation would listen to those who of been in hell, and not strive to go to hell.

I guess Pum Pum truly rule some because, eee ha sum aunda lack an key fi real.

But it's not jus pum pum alone. Some women are nasty behind the pum pum. Some do deal in iniquity thus, the Black Cats. Nasty are some thus, *Hell Own a lot of females literally.*

And yes, I did call my nephew and chew him out for his wrong – bad decisions he's making in life. I also called my brother and told him of the dreams, and what I did when it comes to chewing out his son. *Life isn't a joke, and too many people are living life as if they have absolutely no sense.*

IF A RELATIONSHIP IS TOXIC, DO NOT STAY IN IT. LEARN TO WALK AWAY AND MAKE BETTER CHOICES IN LIFE.

YOUR LIFE HATH WORTH, THINK OF YOU AND YOUR LIFE – WELL BEING COME ON NOW. Yes, he or she may give you the SEX THAT YOU WANT but, is he or she truly what you need in life?

What good and true life can you build for you and her, or him in a toxic relationship?

Why live with and in stress when you can live *STRESS FREE, AND DEBT FREE?*

My sanity is worth more than a couple minutes of pleasure trust me on that. Therefore, I've learnt the hard way to rely on God for all my needs. Yes, I've been out of a relationship for more than a decade now and yes; at times it is lonely but trust me, I don't have to worry about a man or woman cheating on me, he or she staying out late at nights and coming in at day break. And no, this has nothing to do with his job. I do not have to worry about him or her bringing home another woman or man's germs to me. Thus, many women stink below of the nastiness he and or she has and have brought home to you. Therefore, you have some men and women that truly do not value or respect the relationship they are in. Nor do they respect their Vagina or Penis.

So yes, the word **_LOVE_** is thrown around loosely by those who only love, _AND CANNOT TRULY LOVE._

When you truly love a person, you respect them; each other. Cherish them; each other.

You are at true peace with that person; each other.
You do not seek to harm or hurt that person; each other.
Your relationship is valuable and valued by you; each other.

Your relationship with him or her have the True and Living God in the mix, and midst.

Yes, sexual gratification for some. But for those who are of true and good life it is nastiness. Therefore, _Black Women learn to value yourself and your VAGINA. God do not like it when we/you use your vagina as a_

Public Flush Toilet. Meaning, different men and women coming into your domain; vagina.

Listen, you are in a relationship with Person X and Person X sleeps with XYZ AA ABC, and more. Did you know that all the women including men that Person X sleeps with, as soon as he gets home, _you take on the Sins of Person X and all the women and men he or she has and have slept with?_

So, because of Adultery; if Person X has unnumberable amount of Sins; you the wife or the lover/boyfriend, or girlfriend takes on that unnumberable amount of sins.

So, let's say:
Person X has:
123,456,789,000, 000, 000, 000 Sins.

Person XYZ has:
780,459,000, 000, 000 Sins.

Person AA has:
123,456,123, 000, 000, 000 Sins.

Person ABC has:
450, 000, 000, 000, 000, 000 Sins.

ADD:

That's:
124, 031, 025, 582, 000, 000, 000 Sins you've just taken on.

This do(es) not include your sins that you have on your Sin Record. Therefore, when it comes to Life and Death people truly do not know the Cost associated with Life and Death.

Now if 1 day is 24000 years in hell. Now tell me, why would you want to take on the Sin and Sins of others to go to hell and burn worse than a bitch in heat?

Now. Multiply that figure by 24 000 years.

124, 031, 025, 582, 000, 000, 000 x 24 000

Now tell me. Are you willing to spend:

2, 976, 744, 613, 968, 000, 000, 000, 000 burning in hell for other people?

Now:

Multiply by 365 days. This does not include the days for leap years over your lifetime.

So, because you as a wife or lover has and have taken on the sins of your husband, mate, or lover; Death can start from the beginning with you. And, you cannot tell Death no. Death can do what Death feel like doing in the Domain of Death – Hell. Therefore, your time will be longer than your mate and his lovers in hell. Therefore, and thus, <u>PROTECT YOUR LIFE HERE ON EARTH.</u>

Listen, it's the ones we trust not to deceive us that truly deceive us. Thus, your deceitful Religious Leaders, Gang Leaders, Corporate Leaders, Political Leaders, Parents, Friends, and more that deceive you, and take your rights and freedom from you here on Earth. <u>And none of you better look at me because; I am not your leader, friend, parent, or whatever.</u>

<u>Therefore, it's a foolish man or woman that would lose their soul for others to go to hell and burn.</u>

Thus, the Bible of Man told you of <u>FOOL FOOL JESUS.</u>

<u>Why the hell would I lose my life for wicked and evil people?</u>

I am not foolish come on now. Nor would God let any Child of Life sacrifice themself for Death's Wicked and Evil Own.

Listen, I am sure you did not come on this Earth to waste your life and or, <u>GIVE YOUR LIFE OVER TO DEATH BECAUSE OF OTHERS, AND WHAT THE WHITE RACE TELL YOU TO BE THE TRUTH.</u>

I've told you in other books. *A RACE AND PEOPLE WHO KNOW NOT THE TRUTH CANNOT SPEAK OF THE TRUTH. NOR CAN THEY TELL YOU OF THE TRUE AND LIVING GOD.*

THE WHITE MAN'S GOD IS DEATH NOT LIFE THEREFORE, BILLIONS HAVE AND HAS BEEN LIED TO; DECEIVED.

Billions of you have and has been given Religious Lies to live by and die by. No this is not fair but, it's your reality when you *PUT DEMONS BEFORE YOU; SELF.*

I so need to talk about dreams as well.

Yes, dreams are a way into the past, present, and future but; dreams are hard to decipher. And even though I tell you of my dreams, I truly do not do so well in deciphering them. And to be fully honest with you. No one can fully decipher their dreams to 100% accuracy.

I was dreaming about my dad in underwear. A red underwear was the last dream I had of my father. I did not put anything to it until I spoke to my younger brother today; March 26, 2021. He told me he has to go to the hospital to get something removed. Plus, I was dreaming about me being in the hospital. So, my dream world was trying to show me and tell me that, *someone in my family was going to end up in the* _hospital._ Yes, I thought it was me but it's my younger brother that has to go into the hospital.

I just hope and pray God stays with him and ensure he is safe as I wrap every positive energy of truth and goodness around him for a safe operation, and speedy recovery that is positive and true.

Listen people, I need my brother. He is special to me in every way.

Wow because I do more than wholeheartedly trust God over all. So no, _MY DREAMS TRULY DO NOT WALK STRAIGHT._

I know many of you might be saying wow she must hate White People. And I tell you, I cannot hate White People. _EVERY NATION HERE ON EARTH HAVE AND HAS A CHOICE TO EITHER STAY WITH LIFE – LOVEY – GOOD GOD AND ALLELUJAH OR GO WITH DEATH. THE WHITE RACE CHOSE TO GO WITH DEATH AND SOME IN THE BLACK COMMUNITY ALSO CHOSE TO GO WITH DEATH._

Therefore:

GOD DO NOT LOOK AT COLOUR OF SKIN WHEN IT COMES TO PEOPLE - LETTING PEOPLE IN HIS OR HER DOMAIN.

A WHITE PERSON BASED ON HUE THAT IS GOOD CAN SAY THEY ARE BLACK. Absolutely no one in the Kingdom of God including God, can deny ANYONE GOOD ENTRY INTO THE KINGDOM AND REALM OF LIFE.

God cannot look at anyone's hue. God can only look at the GOOD THAT PERSON HAS ON THEIR LIFE RECORD.

AS LONG AS YOU HAVE MORE GOOD THAN EVIL, YOU CANNOT BE DENIED ACCESS TO GOD AND THIS IS WHAT BILLIONS FAIL TO RECOGNIZE.

But Babylon – the Children and People of Babylon – Hindu's Persians, Syrians, Ethiopians, Mixed Race Blacks and Indians, and so forth; what about them?

Can they gain access to the Kingdom and Domain of God?

NO. CATEGORICALLY NO. Black People – more specifically, the Children and People of Life were forbidden and are/is still forbidden from marrying anyone Babylonian. THIS IS THE LAW and I nor God can change this Law.

Therefore, THE CHILDREN OF BABYLON HAVE THEIR OWN DEATH; GOD.

Death is truly different for all of Babylon because, BLACK DEATH CANNOT TAKE THE SPIRIT OF ANY BABYLONIAN. BABYLONIAN DEATH MUST TAKE THEIR OWN. THEREFORE, THE GOD AND GODS OF BABYLON IS FOR BABYLONIANS ONLY.

BABYLONIAN DEATH IS FOR BABYLONIANS ONLY.

THE CHILDREN AND PEOPLE OF BABYLON ARE A DIFFERENT SET AND RACE OF PEOPLE THAT IS INDEPENDENT OF LIFE – LIFE WITH GOD. And Lovey I hope I've explained Babylon right; correctly. Therefore, on the Mountain of God, there are no Babylonians – Indians or Mixed Raced Indians of any kind.

And please do not call me racist because this is how I saw it, and this is how I am relating it back to you. Nor come to me and say but you said God cannot deny access to the Kingdom of God – Life access if they have more Good than Evil.

True

<u>*But*</u>

<u>*THE GOD AND GODS OF BABYLON IS NOT THE GOD OF LIFE.*</u> *Therefore, there are no Babylonians or Mixed Race Babylonians on the Mountain of Life – God.*

For many of us the "ROLLING COW;" Cow that comes with fire. Thus, Cows are Death in the Spiritual Realm. Thus, the Rolling Cow for those who know the truth.

Further, go back to your so-called Holy Bible and how the Children of Babylon got many <u>to bow down to, and worship the Cow – Golden Calf.</u> Thus, causing those people to lose their life here on Earth therefore, forfeiting God – Life in the Spiritual Realm more than infinitely and indefinitely without end.

God nor I can change the Law to please anyone. Therefore, people are truly not people here on Earth. I refuse to buy into that bullshit lie that people are people, <u>*and we are all God's Children*</u> because; <u>*we are truly not all God's Children or People.*</u>

I so want to sleep but cannot sleep.

Is my mother trying to tell me something?

Yes. So, I have to go see her soon and bring her flowers.

In order to understand and or, comprehend the Spiritual Realm, you have to comprehend Life and Death.

You have to comprehend <u>GOD.</u>
You have to comprehend <u>DEATH.</u>
You have to learn and know about the different Deaths.
You have to know Symbols, and more.

You have to know about Water and <u>why WATER IS SO IMPORTANT TO PHYSICAL AND SPIRITUAL LIFE.</u>

You have to know <u>VIBRATION – VIBE.</u>

You have to comprehend SEX. Sex is a powerful tool not jus Physically but Spiritually as well. Thus, if you could control your mind, you could control Sex – <u>THE FORCE AND POWER OF SEXUAL PLEASURE PHYSICALLY, AND SPIRITUALLY.</u>

And yes, Sex I cannot fully comprehend, and why it is so powerful Physically, and Spiritually. And yes, there is more that you need to comprehend like heat, the different realms of Life and Death, Reproduction; especially, Black Female Reproduction because; the Black Female in full truth do not need the union of Egg and Sperm to create life; a child, and more.

Michelle

I do not know what is going on. No, I should not say that. I just don't know where to begin with this paragraph, and new day as it's, March 27, 2021.

Seeing faces again before me.

No. This is not weird for me; seeing faces but, *to see Chadwick Boseman's face before me perfectly then, the decayed state he was in.* Wow, because he is truly not decaying properly, and I am going to leave it at that. I know what he is telling me. No, not trying to tell me but, tell me.

More Black Actors are going to die, and for some; *it will not be a pretty death* but an Horrific Death. Thus, *MANY BLACKS DO NOT KNOW THEIR HELL IN HELL LITERALLY.*

Along with that; more Black Americans are going to die. As for his family, I would guard myself from Death because, Death is coming to his family. It's a matter of when Death strikes.

I so do not want to get into the Death of this man because his Death is a heavy one, and I did speak about this in one of my books.

The dead do reach out to me and show me things. This is a fact without doubt for me.

I cannot get away from this because like I said; *Earth is the VALLEY OF DEATH.*

Humans make Earth the Domain of Death. There are no ands, ifs, or buts about this. This is our true reality.

See:
The Armies of Death Globally.

The weapons man – humans design and manufacture to kill each other.

See the viruses humans – man – diseases and sick people design and manufacture to kill each other.

See your Political Leaders, Gang Leaders, Religious Leaders, Friends, Family, and more that get you to kill.

See Politics and Religion including, some of you who are Serial Killers, Hired Assassins, Rapists that rape and kill.

See Satan and the Children and People of Death which are in the billions that live to die – kill self for a place with Death in Death's Domain – Hell.

And no. I am not a Psychic, and please do not label me as one. I cannot predict the future. I see the *PAST, PRESENT, AND FUTURE* therefore, these books.

I do not read Tarot Cards; therefore, truly do not ask me to tell you your future, and what is to come and or, happen in your life Love Wise, Financially, Spiritually, God Wise, Future Wise, and more.

I do not deal in Séance therefore, do not ask me to sit with you and speak with your dead loved ones and friends.

I am not a Spiritualist; therefore, truly do not label me as one. Yes, I know the Spirit and how the Spiritual Work as opposed to what you know. Many things affect the spirit therefore, Vibration, how we vibrate Spiritually.

Water is another Key Factor when it comes to the Spirit. Thus, the abundance of Water here on Earth and in the Realm of Life – God.

Heat is another Key Factor when it comes to the Spirit.

Life is another factor when it comes to Spirit thus, Positive Thoughts and Positive Energy, Truth, Wisdom beyond that of Man; what you are taught to be right and wrong by your parents, the different educational systems of man, the church, your political leaders, friends, and more. There is a lot that we as humans truly do not know. For many, the physical, but the physical cannot be without the Spiritual – Spirit nor can the Spirit be without the Physical here on Earth. <u>Thus, as humans, we are both Physical and Spiritual Beings and in part, this is wrong.</u> The Spirit do not need the flesh in truth. It is the Flesh that is truly dependent on the Spirit. That energy within you that is sustaining and maintaining the flesh.

And please do not label me a Prophetess. I refuse to Profit whoops Prophet off anyone's soul. Yes, Profit and Prophet are the same word but spelt differently with different meanings but for me, they both mean the same when it comes to God, and our Spiritual Well Being.

Yes, you have many people that say they can do this, this, and this, and I refuse to knock them. <u>I am not one of them therefore, these books.</u>

God is not the answer for all because billions truly do not belong to God, nor do God know them; billions.

Did I dream about the Lady of Zion and my brother – younger brother?
Yes

Therefore, Lovey; I put the good and true life of my brother in your hand, and pray that you will keep him safe and secure from the operation that he has to do.

I pray that you protect him good and true continually like you have done me over the years.

Lovey, you know my true love for my brother. Please keep him safe and truly do not let Death take him from me. I cannot handle it, nor would I be able to handle the loss of my brother by the Hands of Death right now.

Lovey, as I pray to you and come to you for my younger brother; please hear me, and truly protect him and keep him safe. Let nothing happen to him because in a lot of ways, he's my rock and best friend as well. He is truly there for me therefore, I have to pray goodness, good health; all that is good and true for him.

And to add to this book on this day; April 9, 2021 as I am editing this book. I did dream DAVID MANN, TAMELA MANN'S HUSBAND. He was dressed in a Black Suit, and was presiding over the Congregation of his Church.

With me being in his Church, I said; "WHEN DID I BREAK MY VOW WITH GOD?"

I was concerned about my Vow with God in the dream. Then David Mann said; "let's praise the lord. Praise the Lord."

Now. I know what this dream mean. Black – Black Suit represent Death for me. Therefore, I was in Death's Domain. Thus, IT'S IMPERATIVE HERE ON EARTH FOR THE CHILDREN AND PEOPLE OF GOD – LIFE TO SAY OUT OF THE DOMAIN OF DEATH; CHURCHES.

I also dreamt the Woman of Zion.

We were at a gathering where different Pastors of White, Mixed Race Blacks, and Blacks attended. This White Pastor had a bad ass child that he brought with him.

At the gathering, the Woman of Zion said; "she doesn't normally attend gatherings."

<u>Note:</u>
The gathering consisted of males and females, and that one bad ass white child.

In the dream. Spiritually, I wasn't feeling good. So, I got in the Spirit and began to say in the spirit; <u>"SOMETHING IS WRONG." "SOMETHING IS WRONG," and the Woman of Zion got in the spirit as well.</u>

As for this dream, I truly do not know what is going to happen in as well as, to Zion. All I know is Zion – Black Zion have to clean up self.

Black Zion must never allow Whites with their bad ass children in Zion.

<u>Nor can Zion allow Mixed Race Blacks of any Mixture into Zion. They Mixed Race Blacks especially of a Mixture of White and Black. All must be barred from getting into the REALM OF LIFE – ZION.</u> They are not true to Zion nor are Whites true to Zion.

The knowledge of Zion – Black Zion must stay sacred as well as, <u>STAY BLACK ALL THE TIME MORE THAN INFINITELY AND INDEFINITELY, AND MORE THAN FOREVER EVER WITHOUT END.</u>

We as Zionites – Black Zion know vibration – vibe.
We know the use of Drumming.
Dance

Water
How to Chant

Stop Death, and more. Thus, Zion must stay with us – Blacks period. Thus, Lovey; <u>CAUTION THE WOMAN OF ZION ON MY ANGER.</u>

If she; the Woman of Zion allow undesirables into the Domain of Life – Zion then, we will be at war because; I will come before you Lovey with my anger to truly evict her ass out of Life – Zion. She and I would be more than infinitely and indefinitely over; done without end. I will not have her compromise the Truth and Integrity of Zion – Black Zion come on now.

Zion must stay clean and void of undesirables – those who seek to profit and prophet off our knowledge – that which we know and can do.

Did I dream the Reggae Artist Bugle?

Yes

Thus, at the end of the dream we were holding hands. His fingers and my fingers was/were entwined with each other.

Ireland, I am going to leave alone. This land is a mystery to me spiritually. Thus, Black Europeans that lived in Europe before the Black Plague wiped out

Blacks is truly not talked about or included in European History, and History Books.

Michelle

Is there going to me more death's in the Asian Community?

Yes.

I so don't want to get into the dream because like I said; Babylonian Death is not the same as Black and White Death. This Race; the Babel's – Babylonian Race have their own Death independent of the Black and White Race that take them; claim their life. So, for me, and to me, *THE HELL OF ALL BABEL'S IS DIFFERENT FROM THOSE OF THE WHITE, AND BLACK RACE.*

So yes, I stand corrected from my other books when I said; all who are wicked and evil die as white dressed in white. Babels; Babylonians do not die as white dressed in white.

To stray a bit. I was upset this morning with what's happening when it comes to Covid-19 and how it's impacted so many lives.

Many; no, *billions ARE HELD HOSTAGE BY THEIR POLITICAL LEADERS AND PHARMACEUTICAL GIANTS – GREED AND DEMONS THAT OWN THE DIFFERENT GOVERNMENTS GLOBALLY.*

I truly do not know why people put their life and life choices in *THIEVES THAT MEAN THEM NOTHING BUT HARM. THIEVES THAT*

BENEFIT OFF THEM FINANCIALLY HEALTH WISE, AND MORE.

Do people not comprehend the scope of the *LIES THEIR GOVERNMENT AND PHARMACEUTICAL COMPANIES TELL?*

Do people not see and comprehend that; *THEY ARE THE CARRIERS OF THE DIFFERENT VIRSUS'S THESE DISEASED; SICK; MANIPULATIVE, WICKED AND EVIL SCIENTISTS DESIGN AND MANUFACTURE IN LABORATORIES TO INFECT THEM, OTHERS, AND THE DIFFERENT NATIONS.*

No, Lovey. I cannot comprehend why *NATIONS TRUST THE LIES OF THE WHITE RACE.*

THIS RACE; WHITE RACE OF DEMONS LIVE TO KILL YET, PEOPLE CANNOT SEE THIS. Thus, *I give true props to the Sentinelese Tribe for their actions – DOING ALL THEY CAN TO KEEP OUTSIDERS FROM THEIR DOMAIN.*

Look at the Black Race how they've; the White Race has and have *WEAPONIZED US AGAINST EACH OTHER.* It's time we as Black People keep ourselves away from THE DISEASED CARRIERS OF THE GLOBE THAT GO

AROUND INFECTING PEOPLE WITH THE DIFFERENT GERMS THEY ARE GIVEN – VACCINATED WITH.

Yes, it's a shame that WE AS BLACKS TRULY DO NOT HAVE OUR OWN BLACK ECONOMY THAT IS INDEPENDENT OF WHITE ECONOMY, EUROPEAN ECONOMY, ASIAN ECONOMY, BABYLONIAN ECONOMY, AND MORE.

I truly don't understand why can't we have our OWN MEDICAL SYSTEMS THAT DO NOT FOLLOW OR CONFORM TO THE NORM OF WHITE MEDICINE AND PHARMACEUTICALS?

No Lovey. Why can't you close off the White Race and Different Races that go into Black Lands and coerce – manipulate people to teach them what we know medically plant wise, land wise, iron ore wise, and more?

Manipulative Greedy Scums that leave Black Lands destitute and barren whilst; they profit off us, and leaving our Black Lands and people in abject poverty.

No Lovey. I am pissed because as Blacks, we are the stupid ones that continually teach our enemies to PROFIT OFF US whilst killing us Physically, and

56

Spiritually. Thus, Blacks has and have become <u>*GUINEA PIGS*</u> *for their colonialized Slave Masters.*

<u>WHY CAN'T WE AS BLACKS HAVE OUR OWN TELEVISION STUDIOS THAT ARE NOT WHITE OWNED NOR DO THEY FOLLOW THE NORM OF THE DIFFERENT WHITE STUDIOS AND TELEVISON STATIONS GLOBALLY?</u>

<u>WHY CAN'T WE HAVE TRUE AND GOOD BLACK POLITICAL LEADERS THAT OVERSEE BLACK LANDS TRUTHFULLY, AND DO NOT FOLLOW THE NORM OF WHITE SOCIETY, AND THE NASTINESS OF WHITE SOCIETY?</u>

<u>WHY CAN'T WE AS BLACK BECOME CLEAN AND OR, COME BACK CLEAN LOVEY?</u>

<u>WHAT IS WRONG WITH US AS A NATION AND PEOPLE GLOBALLY?</u>

Shit I am fed up of SO-CALLED BLACKS. <u>*Regressive Niggers that truly cannot think for self and stop killing self and each other.*</u>

Why the F do we have to build other nations and not our self?

Why Lovey, Why?

Yes, I am mad.

Oh man Lovey. Do you Lovey even know the beauty I see when I look on some Black People?

Lovey, the skin of some Blacks is so Black that you want to eat up the person to how gorgeous and beautiful the Black Skin is on some.

Aye Lovey a life fi real. Therefore, _Blacks are their own weapons against self. We have so much buying power globally that we don't know how to fully use this buying power to build our Black Own; Nations._

Lovey, how wonderful it is to see Blacks buying Black and supporting our own Black Communities Globally.

Lovey, the pride and joy this would give me if Blacks could buy these books, make positive chances for self, and as a Race and People stand with me to help the different Black Communities that are good and true Globally to build themselves.

Lovey, I need my GOOD GOD GIVING COME ON NOW.

I need to give with you good and true.

I need to have you Lovey globally when it comes to giving good and true to those that are good and true; those good people that are in need, and truly in need.

58

Lovey, why can't we build one house at a time.

Why can't we feed one person at a time, and let this true goodness of giving to our good and true own that are in need continue on without end?

No Lovey. We cannot and must never give to wicked and evil people.

We have to and must give to good and true people who are in need continually without end come on now.

As the Good and True of Life, we can no longer build the Wicked and Evil. When we buy from the Wicked and Evil of Earth, we are stifling us; taking away our prosperity. Thus, giving the Wicked and Evil control over us and, we can no longer do this. Let the Wicked and Evil profit, and prophet off us - the Good and True.

Lovey, why can't we come together for the better good of our good and true people?

Why do you constantly disappoint me in this way?

Why do you constantly disrespect me in this way – giving good and true?

Why do you constantly trample me down giving, and true giving wise, Lovey?

You know what. Let me stop because if I continue Lovey, I will cuss you out reckless and rude for being <u>*CHEAP.*</u> Meaning, not allowing us to give good and true globally to our good and true people that need help, and true help.

Stop being stingy Lovey.

Truth isn't stingy, so why the hell are you stingy money wise, giving wise, true love wise, and more? And yes, this is my anger coming at you for being cheap – stingy in my book when it comes to goodness, and truly giving good and true.

Look at the Black Race how they've; the White Race has and have <u>*WEAPONIZED US AGAINST YOU, AND EACH OTHER.*</u>

Why do we as Blacks constantly let their <u>*RELIGIOUS LIES TAKE US FROM YOU LOVEY?*</u>

<u>*WHAT'S WRONG WITH YOU LOVEY AS GOD?*</u>

<u>*WHAT'S WRONG WITH YOU AS OUR GOD AND TRUTH?*</u>

Look at Earth Lovey and how humans are <u>WEAPONIZED AGAINST HER.</u> Earth supply our NEEDS FULLY FINANCIALLY, HEALTH

WISE, WATER WISE; now look at how we as humans are destroying her; Earth.

Look who's profiting thus, who will now <u>PROFIT OFF THE CLEAN WATER SUPPLY OF EARTH.</u> No Lovey, I am getting pissed because; <u>if the WHITE RACE SAY THEY OWN THE WATER SUPPLY, ANY WATER SUPPLY OF EARTH PHYSICALLY AND SPIRITUALLY; ANY RACE FOR THAT MATTER THAT SAY THEY OWN THE WATERWAYS OF EARTH, AND THE WATERWAYS OF LIFE – THE SPIRITUAL REALM AND BUY UP THE WATER SUPPLY OF EARTH, WE ARE THROUGH MORE THAN INFINITELY AND INDEFINITELY MORE THAN FOREVER EVER WITHOUT END.</u> AND YES, THIS SEVERING GOES FOR MOTHER EARTH TOO.

<u>I would never ever forgive you Lovey or Mother Earth if anyone apart from Me and You including, Mother Earth claim the Waterways of Life Physically, Spiritually, and Beyond.</u>

No Lovey. Mother Earth has done wrong to herself come on now. She's made herself the dumping ground for all humans, and I am pissed. <u>WHY THE HELL SHOULD ALL THE GUILTY OF LIFE IN HER GO FREE?</u>

So, no; to me Lovey, and I truly do not care if You and Mother Earth is upset at me but, *the both of you need to respect your damned self.* Humans are not respecting you so, why the hell bother?

Why sustain Human Life Physically and Spiritually?

Why become the dung of Earth and the Spiritual Realm for humans and Spirit?

If you cannot respect yourself; *how can others respect You Lovey, and Mother Earth?*

Now tell me Lovey and Mother Earth, why are there no good and true guidelines set out here on Earth for humans and Spirits to follow?

Why do humans have free reign of Earth to do all that is evil?

And to be fully and truly honest with you Lovey. You and Mother Earth are truly lousy parents. Yes, I can and do say the same for me.

Yes, I know, not all follow good telling I give you both this, but what can we do harmoniously, truly peacefully, truly good and clean to change the Environment of Earth for the better good?

Evil trample down good this I know.
Evil seek to kill all who are good this I know.

Evil cannot live with good this I know.
Evil cannot be clean this I know.

But what I truly do not know is, **WHY EARTH?**

WHY SABOTAGE EARTH?
WHY SACRIFICE EARTH?

Meaning, why is Earth sacrificing herself to keep all that is wicked and evil in her?

Maybe it's not for me to know, but Lovey, I truly need out of this cruel environment. I know there is a better way, but how do I get to this better way?

Does the mind not trap you in the confines of hell?

Does the mind not do all to prevent you from reaching your true potential Spiritually here on Earth?

Is this Earth not a prison that humans no matter the Energy Flow cannot escape?

Is Earth not dirty that You Lovey refuse to come back into Earth? Thus, making Earth like unto Sodom and Gomorrah of man's so-called Holy Book – Bible.

Look how much Death is in Earth Lovey.

Now tell me. Who can reach you spiritually as they are?

Therefore, Cleanliness is important to Life as well. Without Cleanliness and Truth, you cannot fully comprehend Life Lovey come on now. Therefore, Truth requires Cleanliness, and Cleanliness requires Truth – You Lovey.

Michelle

Yesterday and this morning March 29, 2021 I reached my breaking point Spiritually, Life Wise, Death Wise, Mate Wise, God Wise, and Earth Wise with God and Earth to the point where; I told off God and Earth. *Was that a big mistake on my part?*

Categorically yes.

Oh man to the hell that was unleashed on me Death Wise. My Blood Pressure escalated to the point of where I thought I was going to have a Heart Attack due to the pressure I was feeling.

The amount of Death that was around me; my sleep was hell, and now I am miserable to the point of; if anything goes wrong....no. I walked my dog and the second one wanted to go out but I could not take her. It's too cold outside, and I refuse to take her out. I refuse to feed them and water them. I have kids in the house and my lazy daughter refuses to walk any of the dogs. *If I talk to her, I am annoying her.* It's like you know what, I wish I had my own house somewhere warm all year round and they can't get to me because this time around, I want no children living with me. They are old enough to be on their own. Yes, I will miss them but; as long as I am happy, I am okay. Too old and tired to be living a ghetto life that is not going anywhere Life Wise, Health Wise, and more right now. And I know this is me talking but I truly need an escape to some warm island for about a week. Yes, all inclusive where I don't have to think of the world, my life, and the happenings going on in the world, and my life.

Yes, it's a complaining morning for me as it's, *JUST ONE OF THOSE DAYS WHERE I TRULY DON'T BLEEPING CARE FOR ANYTHING.*

I truly don't care if God is pleased with me because, *I am truly not pleased with God living in HIS SLAVERY, SPIRITUALLY AND PHYSICALLY.*

I truly don't care for Mother Earth either. Humans have and has done enough damage in her that I truly don't think she can recover nor, *do I care if she recovers from the onslaught of damage humans has and have done in her and to her because; she's too stupid anyway.* Why the hell should I care and worry about her?

Let humans continue to use and abuse her. She's too stupid to see the damage that is being done in her and to her.

She's in an Abusive Relationship all around with humans, and she's too dumb to walk away from the bullshit of her Abusers – Humans.

Humans want to kill her let them. I truly don't care this morning because, I have and has reached my breaking point with God, and Mother Earth.

To the way I feel right now. F both of them.

No, don't be shocked. I do get days like these where anything goes. I truly don't bleeping care.

Don't care if the world come to an end right now.

Don't care how White People – all humans destroy Earth right now.

Don't care how White People kill people right now.
Don't care how people kill people right now.
This is a low day for me, and I am venting my way.

God and Earth are not right for me right now.
My spirit truly don't care.
I truly don't care.

Bleep Life and all that's in Life I say right now.

There are days when I get tired of my Life, and today is just one of those days where I am tired of Life.

Tired of God and wish I was in the Realm of NO GOD.

That Realm where I don't have to think about God because all is pure and true; void of God, and the bullshit surrounding God, and the Spiritual Realm.

That Realm where absolute true peace exist. Therefore, I need to get out of this God Stage of Life and True Love.

In life, ONE CANNOT LOVE TRUE AND THE OTHER LOVE SO. IT JUST DOES NOT WORK

FOR ME. I AM GIVING MY LIFE AWAY IN VAIN.

Truly loving God for me is painful at times because; *WHAT I AM LOOKING FOR IN GOD IT IS TRULY NOT THERE.*

Going around in circles with God is truly not for me. I truly do not need an uneven pathway with God. I need a truly even pathway that is not filled with pitfalls and disappoint. Therefore, my life with God is truly not life it's Death.

I cannot continue to give truth, and get naught back in return. I am tired of making excuses in life for a God that truly do not work for me all around.

Protection God is great at. I will not take that from God, but Life Wise, and what I truly need for me and God, God is truly not there. I am not truly encouraged by God.

Yes, I write, but there is something truly missing with me and God. There's this void that I cannot get beyond on some days. So no, my journey with God is truly not cut and dry. My journey is paved with heartache and pain.

I do not know what is going to happen globally Job Wise after they; *the Global Leaders, and the Corporate Greed of Wickedness and Deceit let up on this Pandemic,* but something is truly not good when it comes to White People, *and the games they are playing with the lives of billions globally.*

And before I continue on. Let me interrupt this book before I forget.

It's April 06, 2021, and I am dreaming about Children. Mexican Children and Starvation. So, I truly do not know what is going on in Mexico right now Food Wise.

Did I dream about Jet Lee and Chinese Food – Chinese Restaurant the day before?

Yes

<u>*In the dream, someone was poisoning Jet Lee, and he died.*</u> So, with this Pandemic, I have to watch the Lies the North American Hemisphere – America and Canada spread about China and or, the Mongolian Nation Globally for people to further lash out and blame them for this Virus America and Canada designed in labs and bring to other nations to infect them then blame them that nation; China for spreading diseases.

<u>*Did America not do this – Lie on Africa when it came to AIDS and EBOLA?*</u> Diseases they design and manufacture to kill nations and, <u>*STUPID BLACKS GLOBALLY ARE NOT WAKING UP TO THE LIES AND DECEIT, AND THE KILLINGS THE WHITE RACE DO INTENTIONALLY GLOBALLY TO WIPE OUT; KILL NATIONS.*</u> *Therefore, humans are*

controlled <u>*Psychologically by Lies – WHITE*</u>
<u>*LIES.*</u>

Now tell me. How the hell did this Race; "the White
Race" become the dominant race of evil, <u>and people</u>
<u>just follow behind them like lambs going to the</u>
<u>Slaughterhouse of Death?</u>

When did God say, the White Race is the superior race
so, however they kill billions is truly up to them; I give
permission for the White Race to kill by any means
necessary?

How the hell did the White Race gain access to all
thus, <u>billions bow down to their evil will; lies?</u>

I truly do not know how the world is going to cope
because; <u>*"THE GRASS IS TRULY NOT*</u>
<u>*GREENER ON THE OTHER SIDE FOR REAL."*</u>

I cannot fully tell you this dream I had because, it had
to do with this Young White Female. We were lovers,
and I was feeling up her small taa taas. But what I
saw was not pretty thus the greenery –
disappointment in life when it comes to White People.
And no, I am so not going to worry about the
Economics of the Global Marketplace Job Wise. Things
are truly not going to be the same. Jobs are scarce right
now, and it's only going to get worse from the dream.
Unless we as people start thinking for self and see
what is happening around us and start doing to help

self by getting rid of all the negatives – our life; things will never change here on Earth. <u>The White Race – White People will continue to lie and deceive as well as, kill.</u>

All that is happening here on Earth is killing us. If we do not change the negatives in our life, we cannot truly live.

Death isn't just physical.

"DEATH IS SPIRITUAL ALSO."

BOB MARLEY DREAM/VISION

Dreamt Bob Marley again.

The dream had to do with his grand children. Something is going to happen to one of them. The one that was shown to me in my dream was Jo Mersa Marley. I truly do not know if he's going to die or get hurt, but their grandfather is showing me his grandchildren. So, the Marley's have to be careful especially the grand kids.

Could I let go of this dream that was more like a vision?

No

<u>I could not get away from this dream. I was being reminded virtually all night when it comes to Bob Marley's grandchildren. Bob would not let me go of</u>

his dream/vision. So, the Marley's – Marley Grandchildren are being warned.

Did I dream see my mother – dead mother?

Yes

I have to go up and see her – put flowers on her grave, and I will do this when it gets warmer.

Right now, I know she's not pleased with me, but it cannot be helped. I too have issues in life, and if God is not helping me the way I need help; *then I vent my way.* Yes, she's been keeping me because this one particular dead refuses to let go of me, and I refuse to save him in death. Let him rot in hell for all I care. The damage was done, *and despite me being healed, he still find a way to find me thus, March is Hell Month for me when it comes to Death, and Death finding me, and wreaking havoc on my Physical, and Spiritual Well Being.*

CHILDREN DREAM

I do not know what is going to happen to Children Globally, but something is truly not right when it comes to them and White People.

I am not sure if some are going to die due to White People, but death is coming to children.

I also dreamt this White Woman calling children Big Head. So, I do not know what drug that was developed in a lab that is going to affect children's head to cause their head to become big.

Thus, it's the sick and truly demented that RUN AND CONTROL THE HUMAN POPULACE OF EARTH. Evil Beings – People that do all that is wrong and get away with it here on Earth, and we the Idiotic Ones – People of the Globe let these "DRANGCROWS" get away with it.

Stop trusting the Wicked and Evil to have your back. "ALL THEY ARE DOING IS USING YOU AS THEIR DUMPING GROUND, AND SACRIFICE UNTO DEATH."

So yes, this morning I went all out with my cussing of God and Earth. It is ridiculous what humans do to each other. Yes, I should not concern myself with this but I cannot help it. I truly do not want or need to live amongst the Wicked and Evil of Life – this Earth.

There is a better way, but I have absolutely no access to this better way.

I cannot live with and amongst death anymore. It is getting to me because when too much dead come around me, I do feel it. The dead do affect my body especially him.

I do not know what I can do to let certain dead not bother me, and no matter how I look to God for answers there's none coming.

Why do I have to attract so much dead?
Why is it that the dead seem to want to find me?
<u>*Am I the Saving Grace for the dead?*</u>

I need a break from the onslaught of death – the dead. Therefore, at times; I feel as if I am cursed.

Yes, I see things but, in seeing things; certain things do play havoc on your Spiritual and Physical Life including, your Psychological Well Being Mentally.

So, for those of you who are saying; I am lucky because I can see into the Past, Present, and Future. I am truly not lucky in my view. I see a lot, and Death know me, but in Death knowing me, <u>*Death plays havoc on my life.*</u>

Seeing gross faces at times before you is truly not nice. Therefore, I see horror, the horrible way some are going to die before they die.

And no, I do not need a hotline to every human on the face of this planet. Nor do I want every human to have my phone number. I am trying to run away, and be in my own little world where I do not have to see the happenings of this Earth; that which is to come.

I need to find me and my place before further chaos happen here on Earth because; for a surety, there is going to be shortage of food and water.

I told you about jobs above thus, people are going to become prisoners.

People are going to walk around with a chip in them where they are going to be controlled. There is no getting around this because, *we know those who run things have to control you.*

They have to tell you what to do.
When to do it.
How to do it.

Thus, *this Pandemic was their test run to see how far they will go.*

Mass eradication but not one of you are seeing it.

Population Control.

One Race having total Control and Dominion of Earth – You the people.

Genetic Control.
Genetic Lies, and more.

So, how do we balance life here on Earth when everything is wrong and going wrong? One race taking full control of nations. Some eliminating at will, and it's okay for billions. But this is truly not okay for me and to me.

What makes one race better than the next?

Yes, we have different gods and views but, what makes Death the best choice for all *when not all is of Death, or want, or need Death around them, or in their life?*

The White Race have and has Crippled Nations. Now look at how Earth is being run. All that is being done is done in the Name of Control – Power; Dominion that take away your Basic Fundamental Human Rights, and GOD GIVEN RIGHT TO BE FREE TO LIVE A PEACEFUL, AND CONFLICT FREE LIFE HERE ON EARTH.

Humans have no say because the Government has and have taken your LEGAL RIGHT TO LIFE FROM YOU, and none of you in Society is seeing this.

As a Citizen where are your God given legal right and rights to live?

Now let me ask you this. *What Government gave birth to you?*

What Government gave you life or can give you life?

<u>So, why are you as Citizens giving up your rights to life; live free of Lies and Deceit here on Earth?</u>

<u>Why are you as Citizens letting your Government Officials - the ones you elect to oversee you good and true imprisoning you?</u>

Thus; as humans, you cannot run to God because, you allow the Children and People of Death to take your God Rights, Legal Rights, Moral Rights, Moral Values, Truth, Family Values, and more from you. Therefore, I am not afraid to tell any Government Official to F themself. They're all beasts of the worst kind, and I have absolutely no respect for any.

Truss mi. If I could command all di Drangcrow dem of the world to squawk and vomit at every Politician of Evil and Wickedness, and Corporate Greed - Corporate Owners of Evil and Wickedness I would. But I cannot blame the Politicians and Corporate Greed - owners alone for all the issues; problems humans face globally. I have blame you - us as Citizens as well. Many of you were the ones to elect Evil Beings to oversee the lots of you.

Also, <u>we are the ones to support Corporate Greed financially.</u> So, however evil - your Corporate Greed - Owners, and Political Demons - Devils use and kill many of you, it is well deserved. Many of you do not think of your life, the life of your children, and future generations. Thus, <u>humans globally are/is like MOTHER EARTH. USED AND ABUSED BY THE WICKED AND EVIL OF EARTH THAT YOU THE PEOPLE PUT ABOVE YOU AND YOUR LIFE.</u>

The Spiritual you can say is no different from the Physical but; in many ways, <u>*the Spiritual is different.*</u> It is us as humans that truly do not know how the Spiritual work because, <u>*billions cannot see beyond the Physical*</u> – what we see, and have here on Earth.

<u>Therefore, the Mind is extremely powerful, and cannot be controlled.</u>

Humans are capable of Good or Evil. We have both within our Spiritual and Physical DNA with Evil being the more powerful of the two. And yes, you can disagree with me.

Here on Earth, we are bombarded with all that is evil. Our thought process is conditioned for evil in my view. Thus, Death is pushed here on Earth.

Humans live to kill.
Humans design to manipulate.
Humans design to control others.

Humans design, and manufacture weapons and viruses to kill, and do kill.

The heart of many is conditioned to control; take things as far as they can go without the thought of the consequences of their actions. _Therefore, laws are put in place to protect the evil of life._ Just look at who run the different countries; nations globally.

What does all of this have to do with the Spiritual Realm?

I don't know yet, I know.

Balance
Thought
Life
Vibration
Positive thoughts
Positive vibration
Positive living
Life and Death
More

Now if I was to tell you, Earth can change for the better; what would you say apart from; how?

Life and Death exist here on Earth.

Now the how.

How can you change Earth without cleansing Earth by getting rid of all the evil in her?

How do you go about doing this, without the consent of Earth, and Earth telling Death she no longer want the Children and People of Death in her including, not wanting Evil Spirits and Beings to enter her for the sole purpose of evil – death?

Death will never concede to this because; as there is life there must be Death, but does Death have to be?

Yes, just as there is Life; *there doesn't have to be Death.*

Death is due to humans not God.

And I want to leave things here because; due to the ills and lies of humans *DEATH CANNOT DIE.*

DEATH DID GAIN LIFE BECAUSE OF HUMANS. SOME SINS ARE ETERNAL. Meaning, once the spirit shed the flesh of some, some must spend forever ever burning in hell without end.

Oh God, I cannot continue on with this book therefore, I want and need to end this book here. I don't think I've done a good job when it comes to writing about the Mind and Spirituality. I did make my anger of what is happening globally affect me. Thus, *you see that absolutely no one can control their mind.*

Our environment – the environment we live in affect us, and our thoughts – mind.

The mind do stray, and it's hard to focus your mind. Therefore, because of the Spiritual and Physical, the mind cannot be controlled. Humans are not pure beings that are void of all ills.

<u>*SINS DO AFFECT OUR SPIRITUAL WELL BEING.*</u> Therefore, Evil do enter Earth due to humans, and the Collective of Sins. Meaning, the ills and sins of all humans globally.

Michelle

Seeing so many things. I had to call my brother this morning. I dreamt he died, and it affected me tremendously. In many ways, I cannot do without my brother because; he is a vital part of my life, world, and sanity.

I told him of the dream, and he smiled. I told him it's not a joke. I told him how I felt about him.

Things are happening in my life right now. My daughter fell yesterday and hurt herself. I was not home with her nor was her brothers. I would not say it's weird because, I've been dreaming my mother a lot as well as, dreaming about her father. The one that refuses to leave me in death, and I refuse to save his ass in life. I went through hell with him in the living, and in death I am still going through hell. Therefore, there is absolutely no forgiveness for me for him period so he might as well stop bothering me.

As for the White Race of Demons, I worry not about them. I know for a fact they are not Lovey Bound. My concern and anger now is why God – Lovey and Earth not evict this Demonic Race out of, and off Earth?

No. All Evil is locked out of the Realm of Life – God in the Spiritual Realm, and I truly do not know why God and Mother Earth do not separate Earth in this way. Truly separate Good from Evil here on Earth. Death can have their wicked and evil own. Therefore, in my view. God and Mother Earth should not feed the children and People Death. Death is their God, let

Death take them to the Domain of Death and tend to them – feed them period. But then, God and Mother Earth is truly not like me when it comes to the Wicked and Evil. Yes, my true vengeance.

As for him. <u>*Burn in hell period.*</u> I will not save you from hell. F You period. To my vengeance, <u>*your hell is not hot enough for me.*</u> Knowing what I know about Life and Death, I am truly not forgiving period. I did not have to face hell here on Earth that way. Therefore people; <u>LISTEN TO GOD AND THE TRUTH GOD IS SHOWING YOU IN LIFE.</u>

<u>LEARN TO RELY ON GOD FOR THE TRUTH WHEN IT COMES TO YOUR LIFE BECAUSE DESPITE IT ALL; ALL ARE TRULY NOT CLEAN HERE ON EARTH; NOR DO ALL BELONG TO LIFE – GOD.</u>

<u>*Whether you like it or not; billions belong to death.*</u>

There are/is many here on Earth that <u>*THEIR SOLE PURPOSE IS TO KILL. This is their job because, they are of the REALM OF DEATH.*</u>

Death's People do come in the form of Saints, Prophets, Priests, Pastors, Deacons, Church Members, Jews, Christians, Jehovah's Witnesses, Parents, Friends, Family, Doctors, Educators, and More. Therefore, you have to know God and what God is teaching you; showing you all around.

Therefore, *AS GOD CANNOT FORGIVE THE WHITE RACE FOR THEIR WICKEDNESS AND EVIL HERE ON EARTH, I CANNOT FORGIVE THEM; THE WHITE RACE ALSO.*

AS GOD HAS AND HAVE LOCKED THE WHITE RACE OUT OF LIFE, I TOO MUST LOCK EVERYONE IN THE WHITE RACE OUT OF LIFE MORE THAN INFINITELY AND INDEFINITELY MORE THAN FOREVER EVER WITHOUT END CONTINUALLY WITHOUT END.

And to be fully honest with you. The White Race do not need my forgiveness because; THEIR SINS ARE UNFORGIVEN. Thus, they are LOCKED OUT OF LIFE – GOD'S WORLD; KINGDOM PERIOD.

Listen, DEATH IS NOT THE ANSWER TO LIFE.

LIFE IS THE ANSWER TO LIFE.

Now let me ask you this.

Do you think of your Spiritual Life?

Do you think of where your Spirit go to Live or Die depending on the life you live here on Earth?

Are you one of the ones who believe that when you die you go directly to see God, and you're going to live happy ever after therefore, it matters not how much you've sinned here on Earth?

Are you one of the ones that truly do not think of Death nor know that *DEATH IS A GOD*?

Are you one of the ones who do not know the truth of God, and the different gods including, *gods – beings that come in the form of Life, and humans?*

Wow because life for some is truly a game where you are eliminated at will.

Now let me ask you this and answer me truthfully.

WAS THIS PANDEMIC CALLED FOR?

Now tell me.

WHO IS CONTROLLING YOU?

HOW MANY OF YOU HAVE BEEN CHIPPED WITHOUT KNOWING IT?

WHO IS TELLING YOU WHAT TO DO, WHEN TO GO OUT, WHEN TO SHOP, WHERE TO SHOP, WHAT TO BUY, WHEN TO GO TO THE DOCTOR, HOW TO LIVE?

Now let me ask you this.

With people being contained in their homes and apartment. How come the virus (Covid-19 Virus) count has reached record high day in and day out?

Shouldn't the Virus (Covid-19 Virus) be contained fully because you are imprisoned in our home?

"THINK"

Stop letting Evil use you at will. Every human have/has a GOD GIVEN RIGHT TO WALK FREELY ON EARTH. THEREFORE, THERE IS NO SUCH THING AS DEMOCRACY, OR FREEDOM HERE ON EARTH GIVEN WHO – THE DEMONS THAT RUN AND CONTROL THE EARTH – YOU THE GLOBAL POPULACE.

Now look into life and tell me.

Who is gaining financially?
Who is losing financially?

Now look at things.

"WHOSE NEW WORLD ORDER IS THIS?"

Look at the Jobless. Jobless society because; while you are out of work, POINT OF SALE

TERMINALS HAVE AND HAS REPLACED MANY OF YOU.

TECHNOLOGY IS GAINING WHILE YOU AS HUMANS ARE LOSING.

SELF DRIVING CARS.

ROBOTS REPLACING HUMANS JOB WISE, AND MORE.

Soon, Technology – Robots will replace nurses and doctors, police officers, and more.

"THINK"

Their New Earth of Control – controlling you.

"THEIR NEW WORLD ORDER."

Now tell me. WHAT DISEASES DID GOD CREATE AND OR, DESIGN, THEN MANUFACTURE TO KILL MAN – HUMANS – ALL LIFE FORM FOR THAT MATTER?

When did God say; HUMANS – ALL IN HUMANITY, I TRULY DON'T LIKE THE LOTS OF YOU, OR LIKE THE LOTS OF YOU THEREFORE, HERE'S A VIRUS TO ERADICATE THE LOTS OF YOU?

Now look at the Global Marketplace.

THE SCIENTISTS THAT DESIGN, IMPLIMENT, AND MANUFACTURE THE DIFFERENT VIRUSES THEY SPEAD GLOBALLY. WHY ARE THEY NOT HELD ACCOUNTABLE FOR THEIR MURDEROUS ACTIONS?

WHY DO THEY GO FREE FOR THE ILLS THEY DO?

WHY ARE THEY UNTOUCHABLE – PROTECTED BY THE GOVERNMENTS OF THE GLOBE, AND THE DIFFERENT CORPORATIONS THEY WORK FOR?

AND YES, I AM GOING TO SAY, WHY ARE THEY NOT HELD ACCOUNTABLE HERE ON EARTH BY GOD AND MOTHER EARTH FOR THEIR ILLS?

And yes, Lovey and Mother Earth I went there. I should not have but I did. I know the hell these murderers must face in hell. Every life they've taken and damaged here on Earth, *each Diseased Scientist of Death thus, true murderers must face HELL. There are no ands, ifs, or buts about this.*

Therefore, many will never escape the fire they will burn in. Therefore, burning in hell is without end for many because; *THEY WILLINGLY AND KNOWINGLY SIN and, SINS KNOWINGLY AND WILLINGLY DONE ARE TRULY NOT FORGIVEN.*

So yes, Lovey I know but, with me knowing; *CAN ANY COMPENSATE THE FAMILIES OF THOSE THEY KILL?*

NONE HATH A CONSCIENCE HENCE, YOU DID SHOW ME WHITES AS THE SICK/SIKH PEOPLE ON YOUR MOUNTAIN.

Lovey, *THE INIQUITIES OF THIS RACE; THE WHITE RACE CAN'T DONE!!!*

I know Death protect Life by ensuring no one that is wicked and evil get access to your good and true domain and for this, I have to thank Death. But Lovey, can't the White Race of Demons not be more than infinitely and indefinitely shut down here on Earth without end?

Why continue to let them control Lovey?

Is Life not worth it here on Earth?

Peter Tosh – I AM THAT I AM.

Peter Tosh – <u>RASTAFARI IS</u>

<u>GLASS HOUSE</u> – Peter Tosh

<u>How much more stones and blows must the White Race throw before their homes be tumbled down here on Earth Lovey and Mother Earth?</u>

Dem – di White Race live in Glass Houses so, it's time they collapse never to ever rise again just like the different Empires of Evil before them Lovey and Mother Earth come on now.

Goodness is right. Therefore, you Lovey and Mother Earth must come together peacefully, and truthfully for the good and true of life, and evict all facets of evil out of the Earth come on now.

Lovey, truly protect the Good and True of Life because we are your good and true Children and People. Therefore, do not let evil – any form of evil whether Human, Spirit, or Negative Energy move us from you Lovey, or take us from you.

So no, I will not seek salvation for those who <u>LIVE TO KILL BECAUSE, DEATH HAS AND HAVE THEIR NAME WRITTEN IN THE BOOK OF DEATH AND RIGHTFULLY SO.</u>

So yes, the <u>SPIRIT CAN AND DO DIE FOR SOME.</u>

Now let me ask you as humans this.

With this Pandemic who is going to compensate you <u>*LIFE WISE?*</u>

<u>*Who is going to give you back the life you have lost?*</u>
<u>*Who is going to give you back the LIFE OF GOD?*</u>

<u>*Can any GOVERNMENT OR CORPORATE GREED COMPENSATE YOU FOR YOUR LIFE AND THE PAIN THEY'VE PUT YOU THROUGH?*</u>

Have any of you looked into your Government and the Corporate Greed – Owners and Employees that manufacture these diseases, and <u>*CHARGE THEM FOR GENOCIDE – THE DEATH OF NATIONS?*</u>

<u>*Why do these destructive beasts – Animals get away with murder, and you the citizens are the ones left crying because you've lost everything including your loved ones?*</u>

With all the vaccinations that are being talked about. <u>*WHY ARE YOU THE CITIZENS LAB RATS FOR THESE PHARMACEUTICAL COMPANIES – MONSTERS THAT CREATE VIRUSES TO KILL AND DO KILL?*</u>

Have any of you *LOOKED INTO THE AMOUNT OF VIRUS YOU ARE PUTTING IN YOUR BODY?*

Now tell me, *ARE YOU NOT THE INFECTED AND THE AFFECTED?*

Aye yes, *POPULATION CONTROL, PSYCHOLOCIAL CONTROL INCLUDING, SOCIOLOGICAL CONTROL.*

Now tell me. What future do any of you have because soon many of you will become Zombies because, *THE INIQUITIES OF THE AMORITES – WHITE RACE IS NOT YET DONE.*

So yes, *DEATH'S PROPHECY HAS AND HAVE BEEN FULFILLED BY THEIR WICKED AND EVIL OWN.* Billions of you must face hell literally.

Yes, this is your Bible and Revelations.
Your death Physically, and Spiritually literally.

The humans body truly do not need all the chemicals we put in it. Impurities consumed cause our body and spirit to deteriorate. As the spirit is dependent on the body here on Earth, the flesh is dependent on the spirit.

Without the Spirit the flesh cannot exist by itself here on Earth. But, beyond the confines of Earth, *the Spirit can live* – need not the flesh to survive; live.

The spirit is confusing. Thus, it's the Spirit that must face Hell if you have more Sin than Good.

Know.
The human body can cure itself – do not need all the unclean things we put in our body including, the unclean and or, purified water we drink due to us as humans, and many corporations polluting the Waterways of Life.

So no, the Flesh and Spirit here on Earth cannot be fully and truly whole due to unclean thoughts, unclean everything that we put in our body. Therefore, UNCLEANLINESS IS THE NORM AND OR, NORMAL FOR HUMANS HERE ON EARTH.

We as humans keep our Sanctuary – us UNCLEAN LITERALLY. Thus, it's time we stop wondering why God is not with us, and why God isn't helping us, or why God cannot come into Earth.

We as humans did choose to lock and or, keep God from coming into Earth due to our Sin and Sins combined as a collective of people no matter the Race and Gender.

And contrary to popular belief.

"NO ONE CAN SELL THEIR SOUL AND ATTAIN LIFE – GOD."

Therefore, all the sacrifices many of you do is in vain. Thus, all who have made animal and human sacrifices are Hell Bound. There are no ands, ifs, or buts about this.

AFRICAN PRIDE by Buju Banton

Yet, Africans – Blacks Globally have no rights, Black Pride, Black God, Good Moral Values, and Morals. Thus, many Blacks kill each other for a place – their place in Hell to die alongside the demons in them as well as, alongside their White Counterparts.

As I close this book. As people, you have to know. Life for the White Race is like a Movie. All the evils they are going to do is portrayed in their Movies before their ills is unleashed on Society – you the people and different nations of Earth.

This Race – the White Race can be shut down. It is you the Global Populace that refuse to do so – shut this Demonic Race down. (the White Race)

This pandemic was and is well orchestrated thus many of you are jobless.

Homeless
Family less
Godless

"THINK"

Many more jobs are going to be lost.

You will be chipped because, your chip will become your Life and Death Line.

Now tell me.

How will you pay your bills?
Buy food.
Buy medication if you are sick.
Support your family.
Pay your car note.
Mortgage.

FOOD SHORTAGE AND WATER SHORTAGE IS A MUST SOON. Climate Change

Plus, I am dreaming about Heat. White Men telling me about "HEAT." So, yes, I have to stack up on water – drinking water from now. It seems there is a heatwave coming. It's a matter of when. So, I have to start preparing from now.

Listen, all who think they are going to have jobs will not.

No Cops
No Doctors

You being eliminated at will because you are being controlled.

Blacks – Black People think and wake up.

How many of you live in countries that is warm all year round?

Start planting Ground Provisions.
Start harvesting Rain Water.
Start doing for you.

Do not look at the Rich Blacks. They are bought and sold. Meaning, they have to do what the White Man; Massa tell them to do. They have no Soul because they sold it literally.

Death own them thus, many have their *DEATH CODE AND OR, EXPIRY DATE WRITTEN ON THEM AND OR, ENCODED IN THEM.*

Yes, Evil control Earth but evil can be shut down. You do not have to follow the Path of Evil.

Yes, I know evil is strong, and the pull of evil is stronger, but you have to resist. You have to shut the door to evil so that evil cannot get in or come into Earth anymore.

Thus, as humans, you know not the Power and Truth that is out there. Therefore, it is us as humans that gave Evil unlimited power here on Earth to control, destroy, and kill.

It is you as humans that truly do not value your life therefore, you readily hand over your life to Death – the Children and People of Death.

Children and People that are literally killing you each and every day.

Know. If you are not of Life – Good and True Life. God cannot save you. You belong to Death so Death must take you. Kill you period.

It's time you as Citizens of the Globe stop putting your Politicians and Corporate Greed – Owners above you. *They are not God. They are human and they are going to die like many of you.*

Value you and your life because at the end of the day, *you and your life is worth it; whatever if left of it.*

Thus, my world is truly different from yours literally.

Why should we as Black People fight for our rights here on Earth?

Michelle

QUOTES

"Energy burn but no one can burn Energy – the Spirit here on Earth."

"Earth is not the source of Spiritual Energy because Earth is not obligated to God. Earth is aligned with Death and the Time of Death. Therefore, every life here on Earth comes with an Expiry Date. A/the Time to Live and or, the time you live, and the time you die."

"The Death of Flesh is not the Death of Spirit. The Death of Flesh is the Death of Flesh period."

The truth and fact is; "the Laws of Men were not made to be Just nor, can they be Just or Justified."

"As long as the White Race govern, and the different races bow to their unjust laws, ways, unclean way of doing things; Man – humans will never attain peace or true peace."

"Death is not the answer to Life. Death is the answer to Death."

So, as man live unclean, unfair, and unjust they can never attain the Life of God. However, they will attain Death. The Death of Flesh and Spirit."

"Life is not Death and can never be Death. Therefore, many cannot see themself in Life, they can only see themself in Death."

"Freedom is not control yet, many let others control and dominate them."

Michelle

Know:

The White Man – Race do/did not come to save any of you. They come to destroy – kill all of you.

Look at their destruction throughout the ages – centuries. 24 000 years hath they.

24 000 years of Destruction.
24 000 years of Death.

Giving you guns and ammunition wasn't meant to save you or anyone. It was meant to kill you. And, these guns and ammunition is/are killing many of you because globally you the people use these weapons to kill each other thus, permanently taking your life from life – the True and Living God. Plus, giving Death access to Time therefore, extending the Life and Time of Death in the Realm of Death – Hell.

Religion wasn't meant to save you but destroy and kill you, and Religion did kill billions of you because, BILLIONS OF YOU HAVE YOUR NAME IN THE BOOK OF DEATH. Thus, permanently taking your life from Life – the True and Living God.

Their unjust law and laws was never meant to save you but, keep you Shackled and Chained while their Own – Whites go free – spend next to no time in jail thus, robbing you of your freedom.

Michelle – April 08, 2021

Absolutely no one can kill the Spirit or burn the Spirit here on Earth.

Once the Spirit shed the Flesh then comes Life for some and (the) Judgement for others. Therefore, the Spirit cannot die here on Earth. _The Spirit must return to its Original Source._

For some Life, and for others Death – Judgement. Therefore, Earth is the hub in a way for humans.

Earth is a Planet of Choice for all who reside here. Thus, "_THE LIFE YOU LIVE HERE ON EARTH DETERMINES WHERE YOU GO ONCE THE SPIRIT SHED THE FLESH._" And yes, this is in a way contradictory for you and me when I say: "_Earth is a hub for humans, and Earth is a Planet of Choice for all who reside here,_" given my take on Earth, how I cuss out Mother Earth, and more.

Yes, it is us as humans that did make Earth the Valley and Planet of Physical Death – the Flesh. Thus, the shedding of our Flesh. Meaning, the spirit leaving our flesh behind.

Michelle
April 08, 2021

Therefore, not everyone can have life because not all chose Good and True Life for self.

Some must die because, Death was their choice here on Earth.

As for my dreams this morning, April 08, 2021, I will not get into them because I cannot comprehend them. The language was English but different.

The scene had to do with Star Trek, Aquaman, and Hades, Outer Space, me shutting this white door on Hades, two Black Panthers, and my dog protecting me from the 2 Black Panthers. With one Black Panther being full grown and the other looked like a baby say 2-3 years old if not younger. Me seeing different symbols, Aquaman having a cross; inverted cross in his forehead. Him telling me he could not go on and me telling him he had to, me hugging him (Aquaman) and telling him I truly loved him.

In the dream, the Legendary Symbol was used. This other symbol was used as well. Not the Pi Symbol but something in that design without the curves.

You know what, let me leave that other symbol alone because I am seeing the Legion and Forces of Death, and they are powerful. Thus, the Movies. And I will not explain thus, the Movies.

Michelle

BOOKS WRITTEN BY MICHELLE JEAN 2021

MY TALK JANUARY 2021

MY TALK JANUARY 2021 – BOOK TWO

MINI BOOK

JUST TALKING – THINKING

A LITTLE TALK WITH MOTHER EARTH

I NEED ANSWERS GOD

POETRY MY WAY

COMING SOON

I NEED ANSWERS GOD – PART TWO